Bygone Old Aberdeen and King Street

Patricia Newman

Pope Alexander 6th granted a Papal Bull or Charter to Bishop William Elphinstone in 1495 permitting the establishment of a seat of learning in Old Aberdeen. King's College was opened for students in 1509 in what is now called College Bounds. Originally accommodating just 36 staff and students studying arts and divinity, the student population has expanded to over 15,000 in present times. A Chair of Medicine was established in 1497, the first in the English speaking world. Eventually, King's and Marischal Colleges merged to form the University of Aberdeen and the curriculum now reflects the needs of the 21st century. The railings indicate that this photograph was taken prior to 1940 when cast iron railings were removed to be recycled as part of the war effort.

© Patricia Newman, 2023
First published in the United Kingdom, 2023,
by Stenlake Publishing Ltd.
www.stenlake.co.uk
ISBN 978-1-84033-943-7

The publishers regret that they cannot supply
copies of any pictures featured in this book.

Printed by
P2D Books, 1 Newlands Rd,
Westoning, Bedford MK45 5LD

Acknowledgements

The officer holders and congregation of St. Machar's Cathedral
Staff of Central Library, Aberdeen
Staff at Stenlake Publishing for advice and support
Malcolm Strachan for permission to use his father's photographs
Allan T Condie for assistance with transport photographs
Jen and Rosie for help and support

There is a plaque on the wall of the Cromwell Tower at King's College commemorating the Rev Alexander John Forsyth. He was born at Belhelvie Manse in 1768 and baptised on 1st January 1769. He was the son of Rev John Forsyth, of Belhelvie whom he succeeded as minister in 1791.

Educated at King's College, Aberdeen, he graduated MA in 1786 and was later awarded LL.D in 1834 "as a mark of esteem for his private character and for his attainments in Science".

A keen wildfowl hunter, he was dissatisfied with the firing mechanism of the flintlock shotgun so set about inventing a better system. By 1807 he had perfected his mechanism and took out a patent to protect it from imitation. Although designed for fowling guns, the British Army were interested enough to provide him with facilities to develop his idea at the Royal Armouries in London. However, this was withdrawn when a new Master-General of Ordnance was appointed. Emperor Napoleon was sufficiently interested to offer Forsyth a considerable sum of money for his invention but Forsyth declined. Later, the British Government decided to award him a small pension, but the first instalment arrived on the day he died so he did not get any benefit from it Eventually, his invention was further improved to provide the percussion cap firing system. This plaque is a copy of the one in the Tower of London.

Introduction

This publication covers the area of Aberdeen including Old Aberdeen and King Street.

Old Aberdeen was made a Burgh of Barony under the control of the Church on 26th December 1489, in the time of King James IV, giving the right to hold a market. It was incorporated into the adjacent Royal Burgh of Aberdeen by Act of Parliament in 1891.

The road to the north from Aberdeen ran from the Castlegate, up Broad Street to the Gallowgate and thence via the Spital, College Bounds and High Street to Don Street and the Brig o' Balgownie. The old Brig was the only bridge crossing the Don for many miles although there were some fords and river ferries that could be used. Indeed William Roy's military map surveyed from 1746 to 1755 depicted no other bridges over the Don except the Brig o' Balgownie and that was four centuries after the Brig was built.

At the end of the 18th century Aberdeen still had the street layout of the mediaeval burgh and poor communication with the surrounding areas. In the early 1800s it was recognised that if Aberdeen were to flourish, it required better access to the north, west and south. Charles Abercromby, a road engineer, proposed a plan incorporating two new streets – Union Street and King Street. This ambitious and costly enterprise was supported chiefly by Thomas Leys of Glasgoforest and Gavin Hadden of Persley, successive provosts of Aberdeen and business partners in the textile industry.

If King Street had not been built, and the old road merely improved, Aberdeen would probably have lost many of its historic buildings in Old Aberdeen to accommodate increased traffic.

King Street was driven north from the Castlegate cutting North Street in two forming East and West North Street, through what was known as the Back Butts (now Mealmarket Street), and on into open fields owned by 'sundry proprietors'.

The building of the new Bridge of Don completed the road north joining the road to Ellon.

Powis House was built for Hugh Leslie in 1802. The amazing minarets in College Bounds formed the gateway to the house and were erected between 1830 and 1834. They were commissioned by John Leslie, son of Hugh, and designed by Alexander Fraser. There is a third smaller minaret attached to the west gable of Powis Lodge. The style of the gateway is certainly not British and has been called Turkish but the origin of the design is not clear. Apparently, at one time, there was a painting of John Leslie in Turkish costume in Powis House. The Leslie family owned coffee plantations in Jamaica and were awarded a large sum of money from the UK government as compensation when their slaves were emancipated in 1833.

Powis Lodge, at 51a College Bounds in the distance was built around 1697 and has been subject to a number of modifications and modernisations over the centuries. The alterations in 1829 were possibly designed by John Smith.

This view of College Bounds shows King's College on the right. The Chapel was consecrated in 1509 and the choir stalls and rood screen are original. The magnificent Crown Tower in the photograph, has become a symbol of the University. However, it is not the original crown. That was destroyed in a gale in 1633 and rebuilt. The gable of a house on the left with a gas lamp on a bracket above the garden door is Powis Lodge, one time home of the Leslie family. The Leslies donated a stained glass window depicting the three 'builder bishops' to St. Machar's Cathedral.

In 1913 the University built an extension to Kings College to give additional lecture space. It was designed by Alexander Marshall Mackenzie and was opened that October by Principal George Adam Smith. The architect was successful in blending the new building with its surroundings. The stone tracery at the top of the windows on the bay echo the tear-drop tracery on the windows of the Chapel. The crow stepped gables are typical of Scottish architecture of the 16th and 17th centuries and the tops of the buttresses also reflect the chapel buttresses.

Elphinstone Hall is on the campus of the University and sits just off the High Street at its junction with College Bounds and Regent Walk in Old Aberdeen. Much of the stone used in its construction was salvaged from Castle Newe in Strathdon – the home of the Forbes family. Originally a traditional Z form defensive tower house, it was substantially rebuilt to a design by Archibald Simpson in 1831 and then demolished in 1927. The hall, as seen in the photograph, was designed in 1930 by A Marshall Mackenzie, a prominent Aberdeen architect who was responsible for many fine buildings in the city including the frontage of Marischal College as well as the Waldorf Hotel in London. Unusually for Aberdeen, Elphinstone Hall is built of sandstone. It is in baronial style suited to its surroundings. The hall is used for large events and examinations. It is named after Bishop William Elphinstone (1431 – 1514), a founder of the University.

King's College Chapel was consecrated in 1509 as a place of worship for the College. It is one of only two buildings from the 16th century surviving on this site; the other being the Ivy or Dunbar Tower. The Reformation in the 1560s saw the end of Roman Catholic services in the Chapel. All worship had to be Protestant and carried out in St. Machar's Cathedral or in private homes. Occasional funerals continued to be held in the Chapel as well as graduations. At one time, the east end seen here was a meeting room and there are also reports that the west end was a used by the stone masons working on the construction of the Cromwell Tower. After that, the west end became a library for the College. Repairs to the fabric of the Chapel were not considered a priority and some windows were filled with masonry. The photograph was probably taken in the 1920s and shows the two memorial windows to Prof Hugh McPherson either side of the central apse which was filled with masonry. The Pulpit had been in St. Machar's Cathedral from the 1530s but had fallen into disrepair and had been put into storage. King's was given the pulpit in perpetuity and William Kelly had it restored in 1933. It is thought to be the oldest pulpit still in use in Scotland. The steps now ascend to the pulpit from the other side.

The stone tracery in the apse windows was redesigned by William Kelly in the 1930s. It was changed from the style of the north windows in the photograph to a vertical mouchette design. Once the middle window was opened up, Douglas Strachan designed a triptych of windows resulting in the removal of the McPherson memorial windows in the north east and north west of the apse. The central apse window is a memorial to Prof John Harrower. The wooden arched ceiling is decorated with mouldings and ribs. At the foot of the steps is the grave slab covering the tomb of Bishop William Elphinstone, the founder of King's College.

This 1900 view of King's College Chapel looks west from the pulpit on the right and shows the choir stalls and the oak rood screen with the organ pipes rising above. The chapel was divided by the rood screen, providing space for scholars at the east end and for residents of Old Machar in the ante-chapel at the west end. A rood screen was often found in late medieval churches. It was typically an ornate partition with a representation of the crucifixion (the Holy Rood) at the top. The 52 choir stalls flanking the nave and the rood screen are original, having been in the Chapel since 1509.

In December 1891 the Chapel was reopened for worship with a recital given by Mr Nisbet on the new organ. The array of organ pipes rise above the rood screen. If you visit the Chapel today, you will see the fine organ built by Bernard Aubertin in 2004.

Facing page: All that is left of the Snow Kirk or St. Mary ad Nives (St. Mary of the Snows) is the graveyard which is tucked away in the grounds of the University off College Bounds. From its shape with an apse facing east, this would appear to be the outline of the original church. Founded by Bishop Elphinstone in 1497 it was the parish church for the residents of Old Aberdeen (Old Machar) up until the Protestant Reformation of 1560. The church is marked as a ruin on Parson Gordon's map of 1661. Staunch Catholics continued to bury their dead in the graveyard. One of the graves is of Sir Gilbert Menzies of Pitfodels and his wife, Maria Forbes of Brux who both died in the latter half of the 17th century.

In 1892 a chapel was built on an elevated position above the Spital and was dedicated to St. Margaret of Scotland. It provided a place of worship for the St. Margaret's Episcopalian Convent in The Spital. The architect, Sir J Ninian Comper (1864-1960) was born in Aberdeen, the son of an Episcopalian clergyman. This fine example of Gothic architecture is category A listed.

St. Margaret of Scotland was born in Hungary around 1045 to a claimant of the English throne, Edward Aetheling, and his wife, Agatha. She went on to marry King Malcolm III (Canmore) with whom she had eight children. Margaret was known for her philanthropy and as an extremely pious woman. She was canonized by Pope Innocent IV in 1250.

THE CHAPEL, ST. MARGARET'S CONVENT - ABERDEEN

High Street, College Bounds and Spital form the spine of Old Aberdeen, a linear settlement running from the Cathedral to New Aberdeen at around Mounthooly. Regent Walk on the right is named after the Regents or officers of the University charged with pastoral support of students. The building on the right occupies part of the Aulton Brewery site, much of which was demolished when New Kings was built. A brewery was established on this site around 1790 by Smith, Irving & Co and the premises were later taken over by Thomas Marshall & Co who sank an artesian well to supply abundant clean water for brewing. Their beers included "Imperial Scotch Ale" which they exhibited at the 1886 Edinburgh Exhibition.

Facing page: The High Street in Old Aberdeen probably taken in the late 1930s. On the right is the archway to the New King's building. Designed by A Marshall Mackenzie the archway displays the Scots coat of arms as well as those of Bishop Elphinstone and the University along with the motto '*Initium Sapientiae Timor Domini*' – 'The beginning of wisdom is fear of the Lord'. The single decker bus is one of Aberdeen Corporation's fleet. This bus has a 1937 AEC Regal chassis with coachbuilding carried out in Aberdeen by William Walker (Ashgrove Coachworks).

HIGH STREET, OLD ABERDEEN.

Children at play in Don Street, Old Aberdeen. The row of tenements on the right of the photograph is Listed Category C, built by George Godsman, a stone-cutter and builder, to a design by William Ruxton (1852-1921), architect, in 1897. All the houses on the left of this photograph are listed Category B. Indeed, apart from the removal of a boundary wall to create a courtyard, this part of Don Street is little changed from the earliest Ordnance Survey maps. The large trees in the middle distance obscure the entrance to 45 Don Street which is also listed and described as having been built "after 1821".

Taken at the top or most northerly end of the High Street, this photograph shows the area prior to the construction of St Machar Drive in 1921 linking Woodside with Old Aberdeen. It was proposed as a means of giving work to the unemployed after the First World War. The scheme necessitated the demolition of the properties behind the Town House in Chanonry and Don Street and utilizing Cluny's Wynd and the western part of School Road. The old Town House, in the centre of the photograph, was constructed in 1789 to house the administrative centre for the Burgh. The wide area in front of this was where the market was held and the Mercat Cross can be seen in front of the Town House. A Cross was erected when Old Aberdeen became a Burgh of Barony sometime in the late 1400s. The original Cross was superseded by a new Cross in 1540 and after damage during the Reformation and the Civil Wars, it was thought to be lost but a fragment of this cross was found and incorporated in a new Cross in 1993.

St. Machar's Cathedral and the Chanonry, Old Aberdeen. Aerial View.

St. Machar's from the south west with Seaton Park football pitches to the north. The 'H' shaped building at the bottom left is Mitchell's Hospital on The Chanonry. This ancient street takes a right turn to pass along the Cathedral wall. Facing the Cathedral are the grand houses that sit on the sites of the pre-Reformation manses. On the left is Chanonry Lodge (the home of the Principal of the University) on the site of Belhelvie and Daviot Manses. The next three houses are on the sites of the manses of Kirkton of Seaton, Auchterless and Birse. Then The Chanonry takes another right turn into what used to be called Chanonry Gait where the former Cathedral Manse stands. It is on the site of the Bishop's Palace which was built in the 14th century. The Church of Scotland does not have a hierarchical structure like the Roman Catholic Church so, at the Reformation, St. Machar ceased to have a bishop and it should be called the Cathedral Church of St. Machar.

Built in 1801 on the site of the pre-Reformation Banchory-Devenick Manse, this cluster of almshouses forming the shape of a letter H around a courtyard was endowed by David Mitchell. Who was born in Aberdeen in 1731 and educated at Marischal College. His success in business allowed him to grant £5,500 to build Mitchell's Hospital with a sum set aside to accrue for future maintenance. It was designed to provide accommodation for ten 'Auld Maids' (single elderly women) or 'Relicks' (widows), of burgesses, who had to be over 50 years of age. The original layout comprised ten sleeping compartments with connecting corridors in the two legs of the 'H' seen here to left and right. The refectory was the cross of the 'H' in the centre of this photograph with a kitchen and parlour in the two upper sections of the 'H'. Converted into individual apartments in 1924 and again improved in 1965, it has a bellcote and weathervane above the refectory and a sundial in the courtyard. Although it seems very basic to our eyes, this was an invaluable resource for poor women.

Facing page: St. Machar's Cathedral is on the left and the back of the Cruikshank Building, on the Chanonry to the right. The Cruikshank building is now part of the University of Aberdeen, housing the School of Biological Sciences and the associated botanic garden. It was formerly a boys' school called the Gymnasium where James Augustus Souttar, born 1866, was educated for a time. Souttar was the architect of the Salvation Army Citadel in Castle Street. At the top right is the roof of No. 6 Chanonry on the site of the pre-Reformation Philorth Manse. Taken at the turn of the 20th century, this photograph predates the zoology building that would dominate a similar photograph taken today.

This is the imposing west front of St. Machar's Cathedral with its famous twin spires. The Cathedral is dedicated to St. Machar, an Irish monk and disciple of St. Columba who came here around 561 AD The building of the granite Cathedral was started by Bishop Alexander Kininmond, continued by Bishop Gavin Dunbar and completed by Bishop Henry Lichtoun. Unfortunately, only the nave and aisles, the twin towers and the ruined transepts remain of the original building. The building was weakened by the removal of stones from the choir and possibly the buttresses by Cromwell's troops in 1654. Then, during a storm in 1688, the central tower collapsed bringing down the transepts. The south tower on the right houses a set of eight bells in the ringing chamber behind the arched, louvred openings above the parapet. The bells came from St. Stephen's Church, Ealing in 1987 when that church was deconsecrated. The double west doors are used on ceremonial occasions.

Facing page: The twin gothic gatehouses at the entrance to St. Machar's Cathedral were designed by John Smith in 1832 and were built on the site of previous lodges. They were restored in the 1990s to provide an education and information centre. Funding for the restoration was raised by three parishioners who did a sponsored pilgrimage, walking from Iona to Aberdeen following in the footsteps of St. Machar. A wrought iron arch with gates links the two gatehouses. To the left side of the gates is a granite pyramid structure marking the site of one of the wells providing water for the residents of Old Aberdeen. It was described as disused in the Ordnance Survey map of 1899 and was probably built in the late 18th Century when Aberdeen introduced street wells.

The south door is the usual entrance to this and other medieval cathedrals. A porch was added by the 12th Century. The larger west door was reserved for ceremonial processions on Holy days. In the north wall of the nave there used to be the Dead's Door where coffins exited the cathedral on their way to the kirkyard. This area was damaged by a bomb in the Second World War and repaired using stone from an old cottage on Mugiemoss Road, Persley. The clock on the south tower is thought to have been installed in 1799 and was extensively refurbished in the 1970s.

St. Machar's Graveyard is the final resting place of priests and paupers, shoemakers and stone masons, merchants and gardeners. This section of the graveyard is largely occupied by 19th century graves. The brief description carved in stone gives little indication of the lives of those commemorated here. For instance, the table grave in the centre front of the photograph commemorates John Smith and his family. John a shoemaker in Spital, also served with the 92nd Regiment of Foot (later part of the Gordon Highlanders) in the Peninsular War, and received a pension after being trampled by a horse at the Battle of Vitoria in 1813.

War Memorial in Old Machar Cathedral.

The south wall on the left shows the memorial to the officers and men of the congregation of the Cathedral and of the congregation of Old Aberdeen Free Church who died in the service of their country in the First World War. The memorial consists of a stained glass window, depicting the triumph of good over evil, with a triptych of wall-mounted panels and a granite table below. Bishop Patrick Scougal's memorial is on the west wall of the south aisle of the Cathedral to the right. Bishop Scougal was born at Haddington around 1607 and became Bishop of Aberdeen in 1664. He was actively opposed to both Catholicism and Quakerism. He died of asthma at the age of 73 having been Bishop of Aberdeen for eighteen years. He bequeathed his personal fortune to King's College, Old Aberdeen Hospital and St. Machar's Cathedral. Patrick's son, Henry, was also a clergyman and Professor of Divinity at King's College. He wrote *The Life Of God In The Soul Of Man* in which he sought to explain the Christian way of life. He died on 13th June 1678 of tuberculosis aged only 28.

St. Machar's Cathedral, Old Aberdeen. Effigy of Bishop Henry Lichtoun, died 1440.

Henry de Lichtoun was first Bishop of Moray from 1414 to 1422 and then became Bishop of Aberdeen until his death in 1440. A highly-educated man, having degrees in canon and civil law, he proved useful as an ambassador. In this capacity he travelled to England to treat with Henry VI for the release from captivity of James I. He also travelled to France and Italy representing the King. Most of the nave of the present Cathedral is thought to have been built during Bishop Lichtoun's tenure. He was buried within the Cathedral in the north transept but with the destruction of the transepts in a storm in 1688, that grave is now outside the walls of the Cathedral. Bishop Lichtoun's effigy was moved into the nave to preserve it from damage by the elements. On the wall behind the effigy is a memorial to the Paton family of Grandhome.

This is the old east window of the Cathedral before it was completely rebuilt in 1953. The Victorian window that we see here with its delicate tracery filled the whole of the eastern arch. The leaded panes appear to be plain glass diamond shaped panes known as quarrels with lead channelling or cames holding them in place. The Cathedral is decorated with flowers for harvest thanksgiving. Above is the magnificent heraldic ceiling and frieze installed in the 16th century. The south row of armorial shields has the arms of King James V of Scotland followed westwards by St. Margaret and the Earls of Scotland. The centre row starts with the arms of the Pope (Giovanni de Medici) followed by the archbishops and bishops of Scotland. The north row starts with the Holy Roman Emperor (Charles V) followed by the kings and dukes of Europe. The rows terminate with the arms of Aberdeen, Old Aberdeen and King's College.

Below: Looking towards the great East Window designed by William Wilson and dedicated by the Right Rev J Pitt-Watson, Moderator of the General Assembly of the Church of Scotland in September 1953. The window, along with the surrounding masonry, was funded from a bequest by Mrs Crombie of Parkhill House in memory of her husband, Dr J E Crombie and comprises three lights. The central panel tells the story of the life of Christ. The side panels have saints with a connection to Scotland, including Saints Machar, Andrew, Mungo and Margaret. At the time of this photograph, the sanctuary had fixed pews. Flexible free standing pews replaced them recently. On the right is the south aisle with the Mitchell Chapel at the far end.

ST. MACHAR'S CATHEDRAL, OLD ABERDEEN
THE CHANCEL AT HARVEST THANKSGIVING
SHOWING THE HERALDIC CEILING

This stained glass window was donated to St. Machar's Cathedral by the Burnett family of Kemnay. Christian Leslie of Powis married Alexander Burnett of Kemnay in the Cathedral in 1781 and was the daughter of John Leslie, Professor of Greek and owner of Powis House. The window was designed by Douglas Strachan and depicts the three 'building bishops', Alexander Kinnimond, Henry de Lichtoun and William Elphinstone. The window was unveiled in September 1914.

An atmospheric photograph of the west end of the nave with the seven tall narrow windows called lights. They are filled with leaded and stained glass depicting Christ and his apostles. Clayton and Bell, a firm of English stained glass artists based in Regent Street, London, made the windows in 1870. They were famous for their skilful use of colours that would enhance the light streaming through the panels. Beneath the windows is the screen and railed gallery providing additional seating. The central door in the screen gives access to the base of the towers and the double west doors as well as a staircase leading to the central gallery and to the clerestory galleries high above the nave. Bishop Scougal lived in one of the tower rooms and died there in 1682. The lowest rooms in the towers have barrel vaulted ceilings giving strength to the structure above.

Permission to use this photograph given by M Strachan

In the north west corner of the nave, there are two stone effigies which used to sit in the now ruinous transepts of the Cathedral and were moved to protect them many years ago. The one on the right is of Bishop de Lichtoun and the other is of an unknown canon of the Cathedral. To the right is the edge of the beautiful inset tomb and effigy of Walter Idyl, canon of the Cathedral and prebendary of Deer, who died in 1468. The stained glass window depicts the parable of the talents. Below the window is the memorial tablet to the Paton of Grandhome family. On the west wall is an elliptical tablet to the memory of David Mitchell, the founder of Mitchell's Hospital. Above the vestry door is a portrait of Bishop Gavin Dunbar.

Permission to use this photograph given by M Strachan

St. Machar's Cathedral, Old Aberdeen. N.W. Corner of Nave.

St. Machar's Cathedral, Old Aberdeen. The Holy Table with the 17th century Communion Plate.

The communion table with the Cathedral silverware. The most notable piece of the communion silver is the 1620 Danzig Chalice. In 1968, thieves broke into the Cathedral and stole the priceless Chalice along with 28 other plates, flagons and a christening bowl. The silver was recovered by the police in Glasgow five days later. It should be noted that none of the silverware is kept on site now. It is securely held in a bank vault. The communion table was a gift of the Burnett family. The inscription reads – "Placed here to the Glory of God and in memory of Charlotte Susan Burnett". She was the wife of John Alexander Burnett of Kemnay. The Burnett family owned No. 10 The Chanonry for some years and Charlotte lived there in the early years of the 20th century. She died in 1925 in Bournemouth. The two carved inserts on the front of the table are Flemish.

Permission to use this photograph given by M Strachan

The north west tower of St. Machar's Cathedral showing Bishop Gavin Dunbar's crest at the top. The twin towers were built towards the end of the 14th century possibly on the orders of Bishop Alexander Kinninmond. Today, the Cathedral has two towers on the west elevation but before 1688, there was a third tower at the junction of the nave and the transepts. In the distance is Seaton Park, once the pleasure grounds attached to Seaton House. It is thought that the original owner of a house on this site was James Gordon who was elected a Baillie of Old Aberdeen in 1661 and is buried in the Light or South Aisle of the Cathedral. The Hay family owned Seaton House and policies from the 1840s. Sir Malcolm Vivian Hay was the last of the family to own Seaton House. Which was acquired by Aberdeen City Council in 1947 and demolished in 1963 following vandalism and a serious fire.

Looking back from Seaton Park to the towers of St. Machar's Cathedral in November 1987. The locomotive in the foreground was built in 1947 by Andrew Barclay of Kilmarnock. It spent its working life in Aberdeen Gas Works and was named *Mr Therm* after the character created in 1931 by artist and illustrator Eric Fraser for the Gas Light & Coke Company, and used in gas adverts until the 1970s. The steam engines at the gas works were replaced by diesel in 1964. It was kept in storage at Ferryhill before being displayed in Duthie Park, and moved to Seaton Park in 1974. It has remained part of the playground since then, except for two years between 2016 and 2018 when it was removed so that it could be cleaned.

Seaton Park in July 1928. The towers of St. Machar's Cathedral are near the top left corner and Seaton House is among the trees on the opposite side with Don Street and Kings Street on the bottom edge. From 1923 the estate hosted Seaton Racecourse. The activity in the centre is for the Midsummer Races on the 14th and 16th of July. The course was narrow with sharp corners and poor visibility from the grandstand. These shortcomings and small crowd numbers sealed its fate and in September 1928 the last race was held.

In the early 1800s, the council decided to build a new road to the north, taking traffic away from the narrow streets of Old Aberdeen and the Brig o' Balgownie. It was called King Street after George III and commenced in the Castlegate. The imposing building to the fore of this photograph was designed by Archibald Simpson to house the head office of the North of Scotland Bank. Above the portico but out of sight is a figure of Ceres, the goddess of agriculture designed by James Giles. The building is now a public house. Further down King Street with columns from the first storey was a branch of the Commercial Bank of Scotland. It was built in 1836 and designed by James Gillespie Graham. Against the sky, you can see the pepperpot tower of the North Kirk, now the Arts Centre. This Category A Listed building was designed by John Smith in the Greek Revival style. Between the North Kirk and the Commercial Bank lie 27 and 29 King Street. No. 29 is the Medico-Chirurgical Hall or Medical Hall designed by Archibald Simpson for the Medico-Chirurgical Society. Med Chi, as it is known, was founded by James McGrigor and James Robertson in 1789 to enhance medical tuition in the city. By the time of the building of the Hall, it had become a society for graduates and is now at Foresterhill Campus. No. 27 was designed by John Smith to house the city's records office.

Further up King Street there is a 'Bridges' tram heading towards the Castlegate, a 1925 Brush-built Standard Car 114 which has just passed St. Andrew's Cathedral. The porch of the cathedral, designed by Sir Robert Lorimer, was added in 1911. To the right is John E Esslemont grocers and tea merchant. John Esslemont was a farmer's son from Udny and started a grocery business later specialising in tea and confectionery. His business was very successful necessitating a move to the larger premises here. He died at the age of 88 in 1927 and the business passed to his son Peter Esslemont.

This is the beautiful nave of St. Andrews Cathedral. It is an Episcopal Cathedral designed by Archibald Simpson and completed in 1817, Bishop John Skinner laying the foundation stone. Due to funding limitations, only three sides were built of granite with the façade on King Street being of sandstone. It is recorded that Mr Simpson, who was the architect of many beautiful granite buildings, was not pleased. However, when it was built, it was a chapel and only became a cathedral in 1914. In the 1930s, Sir Ninian Comper drew up plans to enhance the Cathedral interior. A Lady Chapel, vestries and other improvements formed a memorial to Bishop Samuel Seabury, the first Episcopal Bishop in the USA who was consecrated in Aberdeen in 1784. Joseph Kennedy, United States Ambassador to the UK and father of the late President John F Kennedy laid the foundation stone in 1938 but construction was delayed by the Second World War and the extension was finally dedicated in 1948.

Facing page: Urquhart Street and Urquhart Road were named after Baillie Robert Urquhart (1811 – 1877) who had worked tirelessly to improve the conditions for the poor in particular in the provision of affordable housing. It was built on the line of the old road to the gibbet on the hill at the top of Errol Street – known locally as the Thieves' Road. Private investors constructed the tenements over a number of years. The Valuation Roll for 1925 shows these eight blocks on the west side of the street but only four on the east side along with garages, a stable and some sheds. The east side is now all flats. There is a message boy standing with some children at the entrance to No. 3. He has a large wicker basket on his back to carry goods from shop to home.

This Edwardian photograph shows the fire station on King Street, opened in 1899, and built of Kemnay granite at a cost of £16,500. Aberdeen has had a fire station since 1762 when it was in Broad Street. The first firemaster was William Inkster who had trained at Southwark, London. Aberdeen was the first city in Scotland to have motorised appliances. The building has been converted to university accommodation and houses up to 273 students. Originally, the bridge that can be seen in the middle distance took King Street over the Aberdeenshire Canal, designed by John Rennie and opened in 1806. This waterway ran from the harbour to Port Elphinstone near Inverurie. Housewives used the canal banks as bleachgreens. The canal was superseded by a railway in 1854 which used most of the line of the canal. At the end of the bridge is a single storey square building that housed the weights and measures office. The grand church beyond the bridge on the corner of Roslin Terrace was known as King Street Church and is now King's Community Church.

King Street Militia Barracks were built in 1863 at a cost of £10,000, to provide a home for the Royal Aberdeenshire Highlanders, the precursor to the 3rd Battalion of the Gordon Highlanders. Only officers, warrant officers and permanent staff sergeants were accommodated there. In common with militia battalions throughout Scotland, other ranks lived at home and only attended the barracks for training. In this photograph, we see the permanent regular men of the 3rd Battalion. The motto of the Gordon Clan and also of the Gordon Highlanders is 'Bydand' probably meaning 'remaining' but more commonly known as 'bide and fecht' – stay and fight. The man standing on the extreme left appears to be a piper. His Glengarry does not have a checker or diced band around it and his doublet will have been green as opposed to the usual scarlet doublet of the time. A green doublet today is No. 1 Dress and is referred to as 'piper green'. The chevrons on his sleeve denoted length of service or good conduct. The man standing extreme right appears to be a drummer. He has bandsmen's shoulder wings and a white horse hair sporran with black tassels.

King Street at its junction with Errol Street sometime after 1951 before the tenements on the right were demolished and the site used to build modern flats. At the top of Errol Street lies Trinity Cemetery, laid out at a cost of £5,000 in 1881 by the Seven Incorporated Trades on the former Broad Hill Croft. The cemetery lodge is in Scots Baronial style. To the left of the entrance gates is a small hill known to many as the Misers' Hillie so called because you can see Pittodrie's football pitch from there. This was also the site of the city's gibbet for several centuries and the gunpowder magazine in the 1800s. The tramcar is a Bogie Streamliner 19 built by Pickerings of Wishaw in 1949. It is heading south with one of James Sutherland of Peterhead's Atkinson eight wheeled lorries behind. Sutherland's transport empire was nationalised in 1950, the buses going to Alexanders and the haulage section of the business to British Road Services. When the latter was partially denationalised after 1951 the Sutherland haulage empire rose again.

A Brush-built car No. 135, which was new in 1929, travelling along King Street on a football special. A track loop was provided along Pittodrie Street and Merkland Road East to allow football specials to unload near the football ground and then return to King Street. Merkland Road got its name from the old Scots unit of currency, the merk. Thus merkland was an area of land that could be rented for a year with a merk. The tenements on the left are still there but the pillar box and filling station on the right of the photograph have gone. The advertisement beside the "Football Match" indicator is for the Marcliffe Hotel. However, this is a previous incarnation of the Marcliffe when it was at Queen's Terrace. It was owned by Margaret and Cliff Jordan who coined the name Marcliffe.

A complex system of tramlines directed trams from King Street into the yard at the depot. Three of Aberdeen's Standard Cars are in view. Furthest away is 1929 Brush No. 137 built in 1929, whilst centre stage is 115 also built by Brush (in 1925) and 103 built by Aberdeen Corporation itself in 1924. The buildings were taken over by Aberdeen Corporation Tramways in 1914 but returned to military use for the duration of the First World War. Today, the site has become the headquarters for First Group, a multinational company with around 100,000 employees. The building fronting King Street still retains the original façade.

The inside of the tram depot with various trams under maintenance. Two of the 1949 Bogie Streamliners and 1929 Brush-built 131 are in view whilst staff attend to axles and bearings. The Aberdeen tram fleet was seriously in need of new vehicles after the Second World War as traffic had greatly increased and little maintenance had taken place during the war. To augment the fleet, 20 new Bogie Streamliners were purchased as well as 14 second hand Pilcher trams from Manchester. Unfortunately, it was reported that the old Pilcher cars were in very poor condition and had to be virtually rebuilt. The advertising on the side of car 131 shows Dulux and Dulite. These paints were produced by Imperial Chemical Industries (ICI) and ther american competitor Dupont from 1931. The tram behind 131 worked on Route 4 – Castle Street to Hazlehead via Queen's Road – and is advertising Murrays Export Ale. This was brewed in Craigmillar, Edinburgh and sold in Imperial half pint bottles with either corks or screw tops.

The Corporation's two venerable tower wagons, necessary for overhead wire maintenance, in the yard at King Street. At the front is Aberdeen No. 2 wagon, a Meredith 393-9, and at the rear is No. 1 Meredith 393-6. These wagons were also used to maintain street lighting. A similar tower wagon would have cost around £500 in 1938, roughly £40,000 in 2022.

Taken at the corner of King Street and St. Peter Street at the bus depot (the old militia barracks), this photograph depicts Aberdeen's last tram on the evening of 3rd May 1958. Special tickets were printed for the occasion and cost 4d each (roughly 50 pence in 2022) – double the usual cost. The subsequent burning of the cars on the line to the beach has been considered by many as an act of vandalism. The bogie streamliners like No. 36 seen here were offered to Glasgow Corporation but it was decided to destroy them anyway. Manchester had created a precedent in 1949 when they had a tram bonfire. John Gibson & Son Ltd Commercial Motor engineers and body builders had offices at 397 to 401 King Street on the corner with St. Peter Street as seen above. Their head office was at Jamieson Place, Leith.

Many of Aberdeen's redundant trams were dismantled by the Corporation itself. Here one of the open balcony cars is reduced to a shell. The roof of a car is lying to the side along with axles, wheels and behind the roof are the metal guard rails from the balcony. The No. 6 route was circular, starting and terminating at Castle Street travelling via Rosemount Place and Queens Cross in an anticlockwise direction. In the background and on the right are the remains of the old militia barracks. This range of buildings housed the stables and stores.

On King Street close to the Merkland Road East junction a Bogie Streamliner 22 heads into the city from Bridge of Don. The Wallace Arnold coach parked at the kerb is on a Scottish Tour. This must be near the end of the trams as a brand new 1958 Hillman Minx saloon on trade plates is heading towards the Bridge of Don. The tall trees on the left stand on the boundary of the extended St. Peter's Cemetery. The area between the Spital Cemetery and King Street was once Mr Roy's market garden before it was taken over to provide additional space in the graveyard. New student flats now occupy the area to the left.

This is King Street looking north towards St. Machar Drive. The No. 1 tram is on the Bridges route heading for Bridge of Don. Advertising on the back of the tramcar is for R Hutchison, wool, iron, steel and non-ferrous metal merchant in Hutcheon Street. Rag pickers were employed to sort fabrics principally for the paper-making industry. Quality paper contains a high proportion of cotton rag. Out of sight just to the left of this picture are two tenement blocks called Hill O Fare. They are built of distinctive pink granite from Henry Hutcheon's Hill O Fare quarry near Banchory and mark the site of Hutcheon's granite works. In the early 1900s, there were so many granite yards in King Street that the street was said to resemble a gravestone showroom. The wall on the left topped with wire fencing is the boundary between the University recreation grounds and King Street.

The No. 1 tram on King Street heads south from the Bridge of Don to the Bridge of Dee. The shops on the left and the house behind were owned by the Chalmers family in the 1940s at the time of the photograph. Mr McGibbon ran the newsagents and Miss Martin had the shop on the right. Today, the shops are fast food outlets. To the left of these properties is Cheyne Road named after Henry Cheyne, Bishop of Aberdeen, a nephew of John Comyn, killed by King Robert the Bruce in 1305. For a time Cheyne was in exile in England but after Bruce won the Crown of Scotland, he and Cheyne were reconciled. Cheyne used part of his considerable fortune to build the Brig o' Balgownie. Beyond the shops is Harrow Road which is just visible. John Harrow was a wig maker and hairdresser who died in 1793 and left his properties in Rubislaw, Gallowgate and Seaton Dykes so that the poor of Old Machar and Gilcomstoun would benefit. This bequest is now a registered charity helping the elderly poor of the area. John Harrow's memorial is on the wall of the South Aisle of St. Machar's Cathedral.

Before reaching Bridge of Don the trams at one time ran in open country on the seaward side. Here Streamliner 27 returns to the city with sand dunes and the sea to the right. This area to the east of King Street is dominated by multi-storey flats. In the distance, behind the car, there are two houses just before the Bridge of Don. These were called Don View and were at one time a house and a grocer's shop. Opposite these buildings there was Hay Cottage, part of the Hay of Seaton estate. For many years this was occupied by salmon fishers.

This is a view of the Brig o' Balgownie from downstream. To the right is the hamlet of Cottown of Balgownie and to the left is the Nether Don Salmon Fishing Station below the level of the bridge. Permission to fish for salmon here was leased by the owners at regular roups or pubic auctions. Nether Don comprised both banks of the tidal reaches of the Don and the coast to the north as far as Murcar and south as far as the Broad Hill. At one time, the house known as Whitehall on the left had an arch made of whale jaw bones at the entrance. The bones were said to have been brought from the Arctic by Captain Forsyth's ship, the *Prince Albert*, when searching for the doomed Franklin Expedition in 1850. The small building on the north bank of the Don is probably what was known as the salmon fishers' bothy built for 'river watchers' or water bailiffs whose job was to prevent the illegal taking of salmon.

The old Brig o' Balgownie, the original Bridge of Don, can be seen to the left of this photograph with the new bridge leading from King Street to the Ellon road in the distance. The Brig was completed in 1320 and has had many refurbishments over the centuries. This important link to the north is said to have been devised and funded by Bishop Henry Cheyne, designed by Richard Cementarius and completed on the orders of King Robert the Bruce. A fund for the maintenance of the old bridge was set up Alexander Hay of Whytburgh and Newton in 1605.